One Word to Instantly Inspire Action,
Deliver Rewards, and Positively Affect
Your Life Every Day!

*From Television's Favorite
Celebrity Teen & Family Life Coach*

JEFF YALDEN

BOOM!

WE'VE COME TOGETHER

For some reason, whatever that might be, we have been brought together in these pages. I hope this book serves you and delivers the tools you need to make that change in your life – to start today to live with more purpose and more clarity about who you are and what you want – and ultimately give you the kick in the butt you need to take complete responsibility for your life – RIGHT NOW!

BOOM

One Word to Instantly Inspire Action, Deliver Rewards,
and Positively Affect Your Life Every Day!

JEFF YALDEN, CSP
#1 BEST SELLING AUTHOR

Published by: BOOM Publishing
122 Pheasant Run Drive
Murrells Inlet, SC 29576
Email: Jeff@JeffYalden.com
Web: www.JeffYalden.com/BOOM

Printed in the United States of
America

ISBN: 10: 1546772197
ISBN-ISBN: 13: 978-1546772194

DISCLAIMER

The sole purpose of this book is to educate and inspire. There is no guarantee made by the author or the publisher that anyone following the ideas, tips, suggestions, techniques, or strategies will become successful. The author and publisher shall have neither liability nor responsibility to anyone with respect to any loss or damage caused, or alleged to be caused, directly or indirectly by the information contained in this book.

In the event of an emergency, please call 911 or seek professional help by a qualified mental health professional or go directly to the closest emergency room as quickly as possible.

BOOM!

ACKNOW-LEDGMENTS

A special thank you to my team and supporters in this journey, Roger Yale for being my writer, blogger, and editor. To all my clients who have hired me, hire me, and continue to hire me – THANK YOU! Thank you for believing in me and my message. To all the parents and communities who've trusted me with their kids and have allowed me to help in some of the darkest of times. To all of you, I am very grateful and honored to be a part of your lives. Also, to my ISI family and coaches for being a part of my journey and bringing me back to a healthy mind, body, and spirit. You will never truly know how much of an impact you've had on my tranformation. You are very special people and this book is a result of you all being a part of my life. Lastly, to my haters, you inspire me every day. BOOM!

DEDICATION

To the four women in my life who inspire me, believe in me, and love me unconditionally every day. Without you, I wouldn't be the man I am. Without you, I would have kept spiraling out of control and given up, but you believed in me and supported me. You are why I am who I am and why I do what I do. Thank you from the bottom of my heart. Because of you I am alive!

MY GRANDMOTHER MICKEY

Mic, during my darkest days you were there. During our phone calls while I was in the Marine Corps - Your words, "Make it to breakfast." After breakfast, you'd tell me just make it to lunch. You've always been the classiest woman I've ever known and I love you so very much. Thank you, Mic!

MY MOM CLAUDIA

Thank you, mom! Our life wasn't always easy, neither was it ever perfect, but it was what it was meant to be. You've always been there through the good times and the most difficult of times. You're a best friend and a great mother. I'm always inspired by how awesome a person you are. Thank you for believing in me and always being there. Love you mom!

MY AUNT DIANNE

You're that second mom. You got arrested for me when I was in seventh grade. Who does that? Yeah, the greatest aunt in the world. Thank you for being tough on me, but also for believing in me. Thank you for being my mom's best friend. Thanks for holding our families together. You're amazing! I love you Aunt Dianne.

JANET

I'm not an easy person to live with and to love. I know. You've been such a blessing during this search for meaning and understanding in my life. Through the spinal cord fusion, diabetes, hospitalizations, tears, all the ups and downs, you've always supported me and loved me. You've always believed in me and trusted in me. I know there have been times I didn't deserve you, but you never wavered in your unconditional support and love for me. Thank you for fighting for us and unconditionally loving me. I don't know how I ever repay you, but I will continue to make sure that you are my #1 and will always love you more than I love myself. I love you Janet! I love the boys too. Thanks Devin and Colin.

BONUS DEDICATION

Dad. WOW! Certainly, I didn't appreciate you when I was growing up and that is my loss. I can't begin to imagine where I would start in telling you about my dad. He's a Vietnam Veteran. He provided for us every single day, even when we didn't deserve it. He crossed the picket line going to work and leaving work every day during the Reagan administration (received death threats), because in his words, "I had to provide for the family!" He's supported his family even when I knew he shook his head and when many men would have walked away. Dad, I wish I could be half the man you are. Thank you for being a man of influence, inspiration, and most importantly, for being my Dad! Love you to the moon and back!

I LOVE YOU ALL!

FOREWORD

Picture a walk-in closet. It's a nice enough place – spacious, smells nice – but it's crammed with so much stuff that no one dares open the door. We're talking art supplies, paintings, plants, poetry scribbled on Starbucks napkins.

That's me. I'm the walk-in closet. I have so many wonderful things inside, so much potential, but without a game plan I'm just a big mess. When I met Jeff Yalden, I started to get a sense of what is possible. With a little discipline and direction, he said I could organize myself into the masterpiece I am meant to be.

Jeff was my Life Coach on MTV's hit reality television show MADE. For five weeks the world got to witness Jeff's magic on camera, but they didn't get to see our work behind the scenes. I have since gone from drowning in a torrent of worries to being a truly productive human being. We're talking a complete 180.

Jeff helped me to understand that you can't let life run you over. You've got to get focused on a game plan. You have to organize and be patient in the process. Giving generously of his time, Jeff encouraged me to follow my dreams back to their source, my heart, which serves as a compass in life. I didn't have to "solve my problems" so much as I had to put them into perspective.

Now, instead of being depressed about school – specifically, not being in one – I am using my time constructively. I volunteer at my old schools and make myself available to career counselors and other staff. More importantly, I'm getting a feel for where God wants me, without all that old resistance.

Just because you didn't get straight A's in school doesn't mean that you're not brilliant.

Since meeting Jeff Yalden, I have made a new decision: Instead of shaping my career around self-seeking desires, I plan to become an art teacher who, like Jeff, reaches kids and introduces them to their own potential. I will sprinkle my approach with all the elements of my closet: compassion, humor, psychology, art.

Is it vain for me to point out my strengths? Of course not! I've learned to celebrate me the same way I celebrate you.

I want to carry the torch that Jeff has ignited and give my students a gift they can use for the rest of their lives. I will inspire hearts and minds.

Whitney Houston was right – children are the future. Their worldviews determine the course of history. It's sad to see the generations slipping further from their heart compass. I am determined to steer the young ones back to the light. Instead of dwelling on society's shortcomings, I am looking for solutions, applying myself to a future where we all want to live. The future is not bleak, but it can be a little uncertain while you clean out your closet.

Jeff Yalden inspired me to admit these truths. I know his book will do the same for you.

Alyssa Williams

Contestant on MTV's
Reality Show, MADE
Season 6 - The Comedian

Interested in Jeff speaking?

For multiple book orders, please email:
Jeff@JeffYalden.com

Join our BOOM Facebook Group Page:
www.Facebook.com/Groups/OneWordBOOM

TABLE OF CONTENTS

BOOM Changed My Life And It Will Change Yours!

BOOM!

Did you hear that?

BOOM is a revolutionary mindset that is about to bring awesome back into your life.

BOOM is a factor and an effect.

It is the jet fuel you need to be able to turn challenges into new opportunities and to reward yourself after every accomplishment and after every plan has been successfully executed.

BOOM for me can be the conscious decision to take action instead of procrastinating. It can be cooking a great meal, giving it my all in my workouts, or inspiring my audience with one of my talks.

What can BOOM be for you?

BOOM can transform every aspect of your life.

Think of BOOM as an acronym: Be Of One Mind.

BOOM! I took charge. I did it. I made that phone call. I asked for that promotion. I became an entrepreneur. I enrolled in college. I finally asked that person out. I spoke up for myself. I helped make another person's life a little bit easier.

This is what BOOM is all about.

BOOM! You can say it out loud like I do, or keep it to yourself, letting it resonate inside of you.

Saying BOOM out loud and applying it in my life has helped me throughout my career. I have been a leading motivational speaker and a mental health speaker for 25 years, and my work has taken me around the globe, bringing me tremendous joy and the trappings of success.

But at one point in my life, I struggled with type 2 diabetes, was seriously overweight, newly divorced – and an exercise injury made it necessary for me to undergo a major spinal cord fusion, taking away my voice for months and sending me into the depths of despair - depression. After all, I talk for a living.

I have also battled mental health issues for many years and I am in therapy. The BOOM is also about my being aware of who I am and the issues of mental health I address on a daily basis. The BOOM has helped me tremendously with my mental health and living life to my fullest. Remember, BOOM – Be Of One Mind? The being of one mind is about motivation, the Law of Attraction, and being positive.

But as you will see in the pages that follow, the BOOM gave me my life back and enabled me to overcome what I thought was the knockout punch to my life as I knew it.

I was ready – and if you are serious about making a change, you need to be ready too.

Before you can bring awesome back into your life, you must let go of the past. BOOM! Just like that. Let go of the past.

This includes letting go of the hurtful things people may have said to you, the trouble you might have been in, or the consequences of decisions you once made that you are trying to work through now.

You need to forgive the people who may have hurt you or said things they should not have said in the heat of emotion. You also need to forgive yourself if you said things to others that you wish you could take back. If you haven't asked a certain person for forgiveness, ask for it if you can. Even if you are not able to heal the rift, you did your part and can move on.

Now is the time. Starting NOW you are bringing a kick-ass new mindset to your life and beginning to live it the way you were destined to live.

BOOM!

This book is short and to the point with no time for bullshit. Either you want to change your life and start living the life you deserve, or you want to stay unfulfilled / miserable.

Listen, I may not know you, but I will assume because you are to this point in the book that you do not believe you are merely a victim. You are a victor. You are not the bitter kind of person; you choose to be better. Having said that, give this book a chance.

I feel strongly that it will greatly impact your life and be the inspiration you need to change and grow. Just remember, BOOM is an everyday mindset – BE OF ONE MIND.

If you choose to stay unfulfilled / miserable, please give this book to someone who is ready to change. Someone who is ready to take responsibility and grow as a person. Perhaps though, you want to give it a chance. That's the first step.; Asking the questions. Good for you. Take responsibility. Be a little better each day.

I care about people who want to rise up and live their best lives. I truly want this book to inspire you to LIVE your best life in the game of life. I want you to be the person I see in you. I want you to rise up to the potential that others see in you, not the potential you see in yourself. We always fall short when it comes to believing in ourselves. I want you to be especially awesome, my friend. I see that in you, and the BOOM is going to help you.

Are you ready?

Let's do this!

CHAPTER 1

Taking Control NOW

DEFINING SUCCESS

Before you can have success, you must first define success.

What does success mean to you? Is it money, a house, or a new car? Is it a family, a great relationship, or a career you love? Is it friends, freedom, or fame - writing a book, becoming a rock star or sports hero - or is it a combination of things?

It could be all or none of the above, but any idea you have of success will require a different game plan to achieve.

Get clear on what you want. This is the crucial first decision that will give you the best possible chance of being successful.

Success doesn't come by chance. It isn't enough just to dream and hope for the best. Dreams are not reality. Dreams don't work – plans do! Make your dream a reality by developing a plan for that dream to come to fruition.

Write it down!

Taking positive action will transform your life and success will come when you follow a thoughtfully laid out plan. The image of your preferred future is your call to action. It will take hard work, passion, commitment, discipline, dedication, and perseverance to make it happen. You can do this. A clear and specific plan written down and followed every day will keep you on track to accomplishing even the most challenging of plans.

Along the way you will experience failures, setbacks, self-doubt, and rejection. Naysayers will insist that you don't have what it takes. Obstacles, trials, and tribulations will appear out of thin air, often when you least expect them. You will be excited one minute and downright frustrated the next. You'll be tempted to give up.

But do not give up. Be patient in the process. Trust the journey. Embrace the challenge and be patient. Stay the course and start immediately.

CHANGE YOUR WORLD STARTING NOW

Do your part to change the world you live in by changing the world within you.

Start by giving thanks for the blessings in your life instead of complaining about what you don't have. Next time you look at your reflection in the mirror, try complimenting the person looking back at you. Stop criticizing yourself. People and the world do that enough. You don't need to do it to yourself.

When you leave your house, offer a genuine and joyful smile to every person you encounter, whether they offer one in return or not. Each time you do this, you are creating a new habit, embracing a new persona, and creating the new you.

Each day I want you to live with more gratitude, more acceptance, more joy, more love, and more kindness. You will notice that the world around you will start to change because you decided to change who you are. This is your new reality.

BOOM!

NOTHING CHANGES IF NOTHING CHANGES: MY STORY

I have been very successful in my work as a motivational speaker and I have enjoyed many of the rewards that go with it. I owned my own plane and a 40-foot diesel coach motor home. I had a beautiful house. I drove a few Harleys, tooled around in a Cadillac Escalade, and lived a glamourous life. I traveled whenever I wanted to and enjoyed excellent food in great abundance. I've played many of the nicest world-class golf courses in America including Pebble Beach three times. (I birdied #18 each time, too.) I went to all the major sporting events I could handle, enjoyed the company of a large group of friends, and so much more.

But I knew that one day it could come crashing down around me, and it did.

I was married to an incredible woman, but we divorced in 2013. I can say now that it was a good thing for both of us. This amazing woman gave me 17 great years of love, family, fun, and growth – but we came to realize that we were never truly compatible.

Looking back at this time of separation, I can see that I struggled more than I thought I did.

I knew that I was mentally ill, but never truly accepted it. A few more broken relationships, hardships, relocations, and challenges made me realize that the real source of my problems came from within. It was a lot of looking in the mirror and taking responsibility. BOOM! I did it.

When you suddenly realize that you are your own worst enemy, that's a pretty powerful place to be. Accept it. Own it. Take it all in and work from there. It was an amazing revelation, but the full impact had not hit yet.

I moved to New Bern, North Carolina from Cape Cod, Massachusetts. I wanted to be closer to my family and my nephew, Patrick, who has autism. I rented a beautiful home on a golf course on the water with my boat docked right behind my house. I thought my life was perfect, but I was gaining weight and my diabetes jumped from borderline to type 2. I was in and out of doctors' offices, but I still didn't take my diagnosis seriously.

I tried to change my lifestyle, but it was just too much. I was able to make good decisions for a week or two, but then kept falling off the wagon. I couldn't stay consistent with what I needed to do to stay healthy.

Because of my speaking schedule, my life didn't have a normal routine or structure. It didn't then and it doesn't now. I am never in the same place long enough to be able to go grocery shopping, pack a healthy lunch, or go to the gym. I am constantly in hotels and rental cars, and it's absolutely a crazy schedule, but I love it.

I'll never forget the day I went over to my parents' house on a Saturday afternoon. I told them I felt like I was going to die and that

I didn't want to die alone. I stayed there for hours, but I started to feel a little better that night and drove home and went to bed. Around midnight, my father came to my house.

"Get up," he said in his stern military voice. "Your mother and I are concerned, and I'm calling 911. You need to go to the hospital."

Before I knew it, I was in an ambulance and on my way to the hospital.

The next morning after they gave me an IV and filled me up with fluids, I felt like a million dollars. I remember exactly how I felt when I saw my mom and dad the next day. I was so full of energy that I felt like I was ready to build a deck.

I ended up getting a stress test, blood work, and every exam under the sun. Everything pointed to the fact that I had type 2 diabetes and clearly wasn't taking care of myself.

A year later, I moved to Myrtle Beach, South Carolina into a beautiful home in the Grande Dunes area, which is like the Beverly Hills of what is known as the Grand Strand – a gorgeous stretch of coast between Little River and Georgetown, South Carolina. I had the most amazing home on a golf course in a gated community, complete with a resort-style swimming pool. I was loving life.

But my health caught up to me again, and I wound up in the hospital for five days.

Five days...

My blood sugar was a nightmarish 550. My triglycerides were a stratospheric 2784 – which put me at imminent risk of a stroke – and my A1C level was 15.5, more than high enough to begin to wreak havoc on my eyes and kidneys.

The endocrinologist came in and told me that something catastrophic could happen at any moment.

"If you listen to me, I can save your life," he said. "If you don't, I don't know what to say."

You would have thought that would have made a difference – and it did for a while, but I quickly slid right back into my old ways and stopped being vigilant about what went into my body.

I wanted to get back into the gym, something I used to love doing. My weight stayed between 330 and 339. My heaviest I was 349 pounds – BOOM! I wanted to start taking things seriously, lose weight, and get into shape. I served in the United States Marine Corps, so I was no stranger to a regimen of disciplined exercise, (never mind the fact that this was more than two decades earlier).

For three months, I considered entering the CrossFit box near my house. One day I decided to walk in, and I felt like I was home. I loved it. The camaraderie inside a CrossFit box (their word for gym) is something everyone should experience.

I really got into CrossFit. I drove the golf cart to the box or some-times I even walked as it was about a mile from my house. I was in such poor shape that sometimes that one mile walk was my workout. Sometimes I had to ask for a ride back to my house and I would use the heat as an excuse.

I was all-in and doing well until I got hurt doing front squats. I felt my spine pop, and I fell immediately in excruciating pain. Once again, I found myself in an ambulance.

A major spinal cord fusion followed. The doctor went in through my neck, and I was told there would be less than a five percent chance of my ever speaking again. As it turned out, I couldn't speak for three and a half months. During this time, I sank further into major depression, and eating was the only thing that comforted me. I was out of work. Would you hire a motivational speaker who couldn't talk?

Reality hit me like a wrecking ball, and I had a mental breakdown. I decided to retire. I wanted to be a normal guy with a normal job, and come home every night and watch Red Sox baseball. I would be a spectator, content merely to exist.

I'll never forget that time in my life. I wasn't thinking clearly. My diabetes continued to flare, but I still wasn't taking responsibility. I sold my boat, my motorcycle, and my Jeep (I have since bought back the Jeep), got rid of my computer and packed up everything in my office – gifts, mementos, awards, plaques – and put it all into boxes. Out of sight, out of mind.

I was in bad shape. I was scared and planning for my early death. Nothing changes if nothing changes.

MY FIRST BOOM MOMENT

I spent 25 years telling our youth and families that when life knocks you down, you pick yourself up. I have addressed more than 4000 audiences in all 50 states, every province in Canada and 48 countries – telling it like it is with no pulled punches.

I made it through The Crucible – Marine Corps Basic Training's Final Test – and became a Marine. I knew deep down that I couldn't go out like this.

I needed to take my own medicine. I needed to listen to my own advice. I needed something and I needed it quickly.

Months later, I was organizing and cleaning up in my garage. I love my garage, and I keep it neat. That Sunday as I was rearranging, I came across the boxes from my office and broke down hard. My whole career – my life – was in those boxes. This was everything I ever worked for – my lifeblood – and it was all tucked away in my garage.

I'm not going out like this.

The next day, I called a local therapist. I needed help, and I wasn't afraid to ask for it. After a few sessions, we decided to recreate my toolbox, which is basically a reassessment of my strengths. A box filled with happy moments. I started to celebrate little victories every day. I started from the beginning where I needed to build my self-esteem and value myself. Some days, I felt like I was at the bottom and getting better felt like it was an impossible journey, but I remembered where I once was and knew, I just knew, what I was capable of. I had to first believe in myself again and I was willing to do the work.

I'll never forget that very appointment where it all changed. It was a Friday morning and on Friday afternoon the BOOM! hit me like a Category 5 Hurricane leaving its mark. Within 24 hours, everything changed. BOOM!

I moved everything out of a spare bedroom and hired three friends to help me put my office back together over the weekend. We painted, put together new office furniture, and installed carpet. I bought a new computer and printer. That Sunday, I opened my boxes, set up my new office, and restored my life. BOOM! Yeah, just like that I did it. That is what the BOOM! is all about.

I was back to taking charge with no excuses and would no longer allow circumstances in life, people, even my diabetes – to stand in my way. Nothing was going to stop me. I was taking responsibility and dropping the BOOM on anything and everything from that point forward.

Sometimes a challenge will come up right away, as if the universe goes to work immediately to test people's resolve once he/she brings the BOOM into their lives. If this is the case, I am certainly no exception.

But then, I started getting major pain in my feet. Both feet. A foot doctor said it was my back. My back doctor said it was my feet. Nobody knew anything. Despite x-rays and MRIs, No doctor could come up with a "why."

This process took over six months of doctor visits and more doctor visits and thousands of dollars. Finally, I underwent a nerve conduction test. The neurologist came in and said, "It's your diabetes." That was it. Just like that. It hit me hard.

It was time to do something, once and for all, to get my diabetes under control – and I knew that getting a handle on my weight was the most logical route. I was going to take charge and find a way.

BOOM!

I thought about weight loss surgery for many years, but my medical insurance wouldn't pay for it, even though I had every medical reason to have it done: high blood pressure, sleep apnea, diabetes, hypertension, and body mass index (BMI) of 44. The most obvious part of this was that I was more than 100 pounds overweight and, as I knew, in imminent danger of a catastrophic event.

But my health insurance provider didn't care and wasn't about to cover it.

I was faced with a choice: Play the blame game and make excuses or heed the BOOM and take charge.

Implementing the BOOM, I took charge, and started exploring my options.

I was willing to pay for the gastric surgery myself – to the tune of $28,000 – but the doctor would not meet with me until I had a psychological evaluation and an appointment with a nutritionist. I explained to the doctor that I was paying for the procedure out-of-pocket and wanted to have all my questions answered before going through this six-month process, but he refused.

I turned to the internet and did some research for a couple of weeks. I went to Florida and met with a renowned weight loss doctor. I also got in touch with Dr. Younan Nowzaradan – aka Dr. Now – a leading expert in the field featured on TLC's "*My 600-lb Life*." Research, research, and more research.

All this research and then reading an article in Time Magazine about Dr. Elias Ortiz in Tijuana, Mexico, a renowned weight loss surgeon, I decided immediately going to Mexico was the perfect solution. Plus, I was saving about $23,000. BOOM!

Based on what I told him, he knew that time was of the essence, and within a few weeks, I had my gastric sleeve surgery in Tijuana, Mexico by the renowned Dr. Ortiz.

BOOM! My life has seriously changed! My life changed because I took action. I refused to be the victim. I was going to be the victor. Take responsibility and take action. Then, watch the results.

The system fought me and made it difficult, but I knew my life and my future were on the line. You have choices in life. You either let people own you when they don't really care about you, or you ask better questions, get off your ass, and bring the BOOM into your life. I wasn't letting this doctor own my outcome! I wasn't going to die because I wasn't being responsible.

As I write this, my weight is down 85 pounds to 264 from 349, and I am well on my way to my goal of 220. Seven months after the weight loss surgery, I am free of diabetes, free of diabetes medications, free from sleep apnea, and my blood work is all in normal range. Can I get a BOOM!?

This was a very scary time of my life, but as I look back, nothing changed because I changed nothing. Before my BOOM happened, I kept the same mindset, made the same excuses, and blamed others constantly.

YOUR BOOM IS WAITING

It isn't how you were raised, what you had or didn't have. It's not the car you drive, your friends you think are jerks, your teacher who you think doesn't like you, your boss who gave you that review, your significant other, or the weather. Realize what part of life's circumstances you are playing. Look in the mirror.

It's you. This is your life. You must take 100 percent responsibility for everything, warts and all. When you do this, your life will change – maybe not today, but you can start today to make the changes you need to make your life better one day at a time.

BOOM!

The BOOM is essentially the motivation you give yourself to say, "Next!", and it's all the reward you give yourself after you do something great. The BOOM is not waiting to be rewarded, not procrastinating, not avoiding; it is taking charge. BOOM!

Let's talk about some areas in your life where you need to bring the BOOM.

RESPONSIBILITY

Your success in all areas of your life – physical, mental, spiritual, emotional, financial – is fully dependent on the responsibility you choose to take today. If your life has sucked or sucks to this point, then reading this book is a great place to start. Your life is about to change, but only if you fully commit to taking responsibility for everything that has happened in your life. That is where change begins and your future becomes brighter.

STOP BLAMING

It's so easy to place blame on someone or something else any time something goes wrong in our lives. This goes against the grain of personal responsibility. Regardless of the who, what, when, where, or why of what may have happened in your past, let's stop blaming it on anybody. It does no good to harbor hatred and resentment and blame others for what you can't control. It happened. You were there. But, you are no longer living that life. You are here in the now, and the moment you choose to stop blaming others or yourself is the very moment you can allow yourself to move forward. Forgive, let go of the past, and move forward. Don't bring yesterday into today unless it is the momentum from the BOOM, and you are doing great things for yourself and others.

SELF-MASTERY AND SELF-CONTROL

These two components go hand-in-hand. Self-mastery and self-control begin with taking responsibility for your emotions and your behavior. You get to decide how to respond to everything that happens to you. You decide whether or not to eat that bag of Oreos late at night. You are in control of when you wake up, if you will go for that run, or if you will allow someone to get under your skin.

You are not a victim in life to circumstances or your past. You are a victor, but in order to be victorious you need to have control and master your behaviors, your choices, and your attitude. Let's not be bitter. Let's choose to be better. One day at a time. Don't overwhelm yourself. Choose today to be better than yesterday. Choose tomorrow to be better than today. Remember, BOOM – Be Of One Mind.

Refuse to complain, criticize, or blame other people for anything, starting now. BOOM! You no longer place blame on anything or anyone else. Instead, say, "I am responsible," and then take positive action.

Furthermore, at any point where you start to get overwhelmed or feel anger at any person, place, or thing I challenge you to stop for a second and collect yourself. Ready for the BOOM here? Life doesn't happen to us. Life happens for us! BOOM!

Everything we go through in life shapes us and strengthens us. Every challenge, obstacle, and adversity is designed to teach us. To learn this and understand this certainly is to put yourself in position for incredible growth and success. Life happens for us not to us! BOOM!

NO EXCUSES

I don't want to hear it. We can all make excuses, but they serve absolutely no purpose. You can't change what happened. You can't change how it happened. You can't change the people you've hurt or the people who have hurt you. But remember, you are not who you were yesterday.

You can't allow the opinions of others to have power over how you feel about yourself. Get over it and move on. Wipe the slate clean. Forgive and forget. The only opinion that matters is yours and God's.

I need your total commitment that you will no longer make a single excuse. Now is the time for forward motion.

GET OVER IT AND GET ON WITH IT

Everybody has challenges in his/her lives, but successful people resolve to forgive and forget quickly. They refuse to allow their problems to stack up and be carried forward in their lives, choosing instead to simply let them go. They turn their attention to the things that make them happy so they can get on with their lives. Happy people aren't happy all the time. Happy people have happy moments and those moments they celebrate.

The discipline of forgiveness is the key that allows you to move forward freely. You can only enjoy peace of mind when you develop the habit of forgiving other people for everything and anything they have done to hurt you.

ELIMINATE NEGATIVE EMOTIONS

The most common denominator for all of us is the desire to be happy. To me, happiness is a clear conscience and the absence of negativity, so we must rid ourselves of negative emotions like anger, guilt, resentment, jealously, hostility, and that stumbling block called fear.

If you harbor no negative emotions, you open ourselves up to a life of happiness and hope. Embracing positive emotions like love, joy, and contentment is like turning your face toward the sun.

Regardless of past or present circumstances, your success begins with accepting total responsibility for every aspect of your life and refusing to blame anyone else.

CHAPTER 2

The Law Of Attraction And Other BOOM Essentials

LIVING THE LAW OF ATTRACTION

Think of the Law of Attraction this way: It's cause-and-effect. One way or another, your thoughts will manifest the equivalent reality in your life. If you put out thoughts blah and bleh, nature has a way of honoring that and delivering those very things. Therefore, you'll receive blah and bleh. If you focus on success and well-being, you open a channel for these things to flow to you.

I am a believer that what we ask for we shall receive. Why not ask for and expect the best?

Remember, nothing changes if nothing changes. Change your attitude immediately and focus on the good things. Put the Law of Attraction to the test.

The old expression, "garbage in, garbage out," became popular in the early days of computer programming, but it's also a perfect way to think about the Law of Attraction. It's another way of saying that like attracts like. Both expressions can be used to mean that our thoughts attract what we don't want just as easily as what we do want. It's your choice. Negative brings negative. Positive brings positive.

Do not allow yourself to dwell on negative or depressing thoughts because we reap what we sow and nature will respond in kind.

The Law of Attraction is simply a matter of choosing to focus on what you want to create in your life.

Thinking about what you don't want brings you exactly that. The good news is that you can change course by conditioning yourself to focus instead on what you do want. The key is to think about how you would feel if you already had what you wanted, and then to do your best to find things, people, and opportunities that bring those feelings into your life.

Creating a new reality can be easy if you allow yourself to climb out of the box you have chosen to live in. Step into a new level of understanding now with the trust that thinking and feeling differently might just be your ticket to fresh opportunities and a brand-new life.

My wish for you today is that you begin to remember who you truly are, and manifest all you are capable of.

SELF-RESPECT

You are a beautiful person. You are smart. You are creative. You have discipline. You have friends. You have the power to make choices and define the attitude you want. You are totally in control of your life, where you are and where you want to go. That's enough to say, "BOOM!"

But here's the thing. What good is it if I say these things to you, but you don't believe them yourself? This BOOM should have just hit you hard.

Think about it.

I can write all day about what I think of you, but to bring about any lasting change, you need to see what I see in you. I want you to know what you are capable of. I want you to see your potential as being greater than what you think it is. Follow the steps in this book, and I promise your life will change, but nothing will change if your self-respect doesn't change. Value yourself!

From now on, you are not going to let people use you, take advantage of you, or waste your time. You are far too valuable for that nonsense. You own you. You are responsible for creating your own journey, and you must place boundaries on the people and things that detract you from being the person you want to be. There is nothing wrong with learning to say, "No."

Most successful people say no more than they ever think of saying yes.

Respect yourself first and don't ever let anyone take that away.

BOOM!

Are you feeling me? Self-respect and attitude (snapping those fingers in a Z-Formation like a teenager with a BOOM!

ATTITUDE

Choose your attitude every day. This is so elementary, but so crucial to your growth.

Like the Law of Attraction, you have two choices here too – positive outlook or negative outlook. You can choose to be happy, grateful, joyful and enthusiastic, or you can choose to be discouraged, cynical, mean-spirited and resentful.

Like items on a menu, you can decide on the emotion you want to experience at any moment, and as a human being, you have the luxury of choosing how you react to the circumstances that make up your day and, ultimately, your life.

This has everything to do with the Law of Attraction: The world gives you what you ask for, and you control your attitude.

Back when I was struggling, I needed an attitude change. I had to take action and approach each day with a fresh, new attitude. So now, I wake up at 5:00 a.m. I'm at the gym doing my workout at 5:15 a.m. Getting it done! BOOM! I no longer feel that taking care of my health is too much; I tackle it first thing in the morning.

After my workout, I take a short walk to the beach and catch the sunrise over the Atlantic. In the space of 20 minutes, I take in the power of the water and the beauty of the sky as incredible colors begin to illuminate the horizon.

Why do I do this? Because I am feeding my soul. I am starting the day with self-care. I am creating a new day. I am owning my emotions and attitude. I am attacking the day with complete ownership. BOOM!

Yesterday is gone, and the attitude that I bring to this day will carry into the following days. This is a powerful moment where I can be grateful to live so close to a magnificent spot – the ocean, the beach, the sun – the tranquility.

It's a magical place to start the day, and when I am on the road, I can't wait to get home to take all this in. It gives me power. This helps me to create my attitude and fuels me for days.

What can you do to change your attitude? Is it people who drag you down? Close your circle. Is it a job that drags you down? Change your job. If certain family members drag you down, you need to make some adjustments. You can't change them, but you can work on yourself and possibly your influence can rub off on them. The simple changes you implement can make a difference in your life and that of your family.

BOOM!

CHOICES

I wear a bracelet every day that says, "TAKE TIME TO THINK" on one side and "BELIEVE IN YOURSELF," on the other side. I love this bracelet and it is a constant reminder to me of what is important. Over the years, I've shared nearly 250,000 of these bracelets.

Think before you act. There is power in those words. Reacting usually comes with regret. Instead, responding shows that you have taken the time to think and therefore puts you in a state of mind that opens you up to solutions. Choosing to respond instead of reacting puts you in the driver's seat.

We have all heard about the value of putting a small but consistent amount of money into a savings account and how compound interest works its magic over the years, leaving a person with a very tidy nest egg. This is doable, and it starts with a conscious choice: save or squander.

How about the choice to drive a vehicle when you know you have had too much to drink? We have all heard stories about a poor decision – some of them heartbreaking.

Mental health professionals say that after a death, you shouldn't make any major decisions for at least six months. Work on yourself. The same goes for divorce or the end of a relationship. Stop and think. Take a step back and reevaluate what is important to you. Be deliberate. Now is not the time for any hasty decisions. There is no urgent need to respond right away to anything.

When faced with a major purchase, ask questions. Don't answer if you are unsure. You owe nothing to nobody. Be wise. Stay in control. Do not give in to sales pressure. There will always be a good deal, regardless of what that car salesman tells you. Read the fine print.

Speaking of choices, I will leave you with the words of a dear friend, "Choose Life, Choose Love, Choose You!"

Choices matter. Make good choices. Think before you act. Ask trusted people if you need help making a good decision. Nothing wrong with asking for help.

THE LIFE YOU WANT: GET THE PICTURE

Visualizing is the act of picturing what you want in life, and adding intense emotion to this mental picture. See and feel yourself in possession of that which you most want with intensity. Do this daily.

Visualize the future you want.

Look at life in the same way your headlights cut through the night, keeping you on course to your destination. It is amazing to think that you can drive from the east coast to the west coast at night by seeing only small distances at a time. If you have a destination in mind, you can get there a little bit at a time, just like headlights keep illuminating the road in front of you.

Relax. Have a vision in your mind. See it. Believe it and just like when you're driving at night and you trust your car's headlights will keep you on course, you need to trust that your vision will do the same and keep you going.

VISION BOARD

Here is a little trick you can do next time it's a rainy day or you are looking for something to do. Create a vision board. BOOM!

This is a favorite of mine. Go to your local office supply store and get poster board, glue, tape, and scissors. Buy a stack of magazines or collect them from friends.

During your free time lay all this out on the table. This is a great project that any family can enjoy together. Great family moments come from doing the same thing together and enjoying the outcome with laughs and memorable moments. Add pizza and BOOM.

Cut out pictures that inspire you. Whether it's that car you dream of, that nice house with beautiful landscaping, that delicious dinner you see in the magazine, that beautiful sunset, or that pool in your yard, cut out the picture and put it on the vision board. Maybe it's a boat on a lake and you love lake living. Cut it out. Glue it to the poster board. What else can you add? Do you love family time on the beach? Find a picture and put it on the poster board.

Whatever inspires you and triggers your enthusiasm and imagination – make it a part of your very own vision board. You can do this every year, or as often as you'd like.

Align your goals and wants with this board, keep it by your bedside and wake up every day with a clear picture of what you are working toward. Let this vision board give you clarity as to why every day you are grinding in life. Let it become your purpose – why you are working so hard.

BOOM!

This is so much fun to do. Go do it even if you do it alone. Just do it. You'll see what I am talking about.

PRIORITIES

If it's important to you, make it a priority.

What If I told you that I had a free ten-day vacation to the Atlantis in the Bahamas for you and a friend, but you would have to be at the airport for a five-a.m. flight on Saturday morning?

Let's say your vacation time had been approved for this all-expenses-paid trip, and I sweetened the pot by throwing in $2,000 cash to do with as you pleased.

Would you show up? Of course you would, because it would be important to you.

Give priority status to the important things in your life – showing up early for work, getting to the gym, saving your money, defining your goals, or spending more time with your family – and make this your purpose every day. If something is important, you will have zero excuses.

It's easy to make excuses when you don't have well-defined priorities. Make it important, and you will crush your excuses and get it done. BOOM!

Legendary Notre Dame football coach, Lou Holtz, instilled in his players a philosophy called "What's Important Now" – or WIN – which is basically focusing on what a person wants to accomplish in life – and the daily tasks and activities that produce the desired result.

What is important now for you to do today? How will accomplishing that task move you toward your goal?

I use WIN a lot, especially when I am home and have a day or two in the office before traveling. When I am concentrating on my business, I ask myself, "WIN - What's Important Now," and make a list of the things I need to get done, arranging the items in order of importance – with emphasis of what is going to make me money now.

Being self-employed, it's easy for me to focus on minor details and get bogged down on tasks that could either be delegated or eliminated. I could easily get lost in the STUFF. There is always the danger of taking too much on and heading straight down a rabbit hole. To keep myself on task, I make a priority list to determine what makes me money now. The best option goes to the top of my list and becomes the utmost priority.

Live your life like you just won a fantastic vacation.

For an in-depth look at priorities, I suggest reading Dr. Steven Covey's bestseller, The 7 Habits of Highly Effective People. I also use an app called Priority Matrix by Appfluence. It's available for iPhone and Android.

PROCRASTINATION

"Procrastination is you being lazy.
If it's important enough, you'll find a way!"

– JEFF YALDEN

I have used the above quote many times in my speaking career, but I will give you the benefit of the doubt.

Procrastination is delaying something that needs to be done, and although I feel that laziness is the top reason for putting something off, there are many other factors and coping mechanisms that might contribute to the decision to kick something down the road.

Here are some reasons for procrastination and simple solutions

 NO TIME: You might make the impulsive but erroneous judgment call that you don't have the time right now. Search yourself and your motives to determine if this is true. What does your calendar really look like? Did you make a priorities list? Did you employ the WIN formula?

 ANXIETY: A deadline looms large. Perhaps your mortgage payment is coming up, and you need to complete some freelance work to come up with the money to pay it. Or maybe you are afraid of starting or completing tasks. I have found that the best way to beat this anxiety is simply to begin. Look under the bed. The monster might not be hiding under there after all.

 PERFECTIONISM: If you think your standards are too high, you might begin to question your abilities, setting yourself up for failure. You might have raised an impossibly high bar for yourself. Believing that any effort you make will fall short, you choose not to begin. This can apply to tasks you have successfully completed again and again.

Use your past successes as a stepping stone. Trust your abilities and get started.

 LOW SELF-ESTEEM: If you don't think you are good enough to complete a task, you are in the same

boat as the perfectionist – and that boat is sinking. Think about people you know who have completed the same task that you are facing. Chances are that they are not rocket scientists. Draw from your strengths and dig in.

 DEPRESSION: If you don't have the mental or emotional energy to start or complete a task, you may be suffering from depression. If you are depressed, seek attention from a qualified medical or mental health professional.

You reserve the right to put something off if you have evaluated all that you must do and have determined that the task is not a priority. This is not procrastination, but rather a good judgement call.

Procrastination can do a number on you in many ways, including the stress of approaching deadlines and guilt that you are avoiding a certain responsibility. You could be thrown into a crisis because you have run out of time to complete your task, running the risk of letting others down. Word could get around that you are unreliable.

Set realistic goals, stick to a routine, and be aware of your strengths. It's okay to say no.

Break up your tasks into manageable chunks. Don't be afraid to ask for help and remember to celebrate small victories along the way.

Procrastination can be a major negative force in your life if you choose to let it exert power over you. You are the only one that can procrastinate about something, and you are the only one that can remove the desire to procrastinate. Get it done.

BOOM!

CHAPTER 3

The Beginning Of Greatness

MORE TIME IN A DAY

"Lack of direction, not lack of time, is the problem. We all have twenty-four hour days."

– ZIG ZIGLAR

I can hear you saying, "Jeff, I don't have time."

But you do have time if you make something a priority and it is important to you.

We are all given 168 hours a week, 24 hours a day – seven days a week.

We make time for what is important to us. If you don't take action on an item you have determined to be a priority, what you are really saying is that you are not "all-in."

If something is important, you will give it top priority and find the time to get it done. That is what successful people do.

MEET THE EARLY BIRD

Five a.m. is when legends are waking up or going to bed.

At that time, the sun is starting to come up over the horizon. But, millions are still sleeping in bed, regretting that soon their alarms are going to go off. Even my dogs are still sleeping. Not me. This is the time where legends are creating their lives.

For me, the next few hours are vital to my success for that day. I wake up while everyone is still sleeping. As soon as I get up, I hydrate myself with 20 ounces of water. I then take to my chair and meditate, breathing with the mantra, "Inhale Peace" for a slow count of four, "Exhale Love" for a slow count of four. I do this for about 10 minutes. Mindful breathing helps me bring my anxiety down, and I am ready to attack my day. (I highly recommend this simple meditation and mindful breathing technique. It's a fantastic way to clear your mind and get ready for the day.)

After my meditation, I then spend about 15-20 minutes reading and 15-20 minutes writing.

Then I am ready to hit the gym and get a workout. Depending on the time of the sunrise, I'll get all of this done around the time I want to be on the beach. As mentioned, the beach is where I go to reflect and appreciate the beauty that surrounds me.

By the time I am done with my morning routine, I am feeling awesome and ready to own the day. I feel I've done more before nine a.m. than most people do all day. I am owning the day and getting my work in, but before anything, I am taking this time for myself. Again, self-care is critical, yet so few people do it. We take better care of things that don't matter then we do taking care of ourselves physically, emotionally, and spiritually. Take care of yourself first. Make it a priority.

WHEN BEHAVIOR BECOMES HABIT

In order to start your road to greatness, you need to create new habits. There is a common myth floating around that it takes 21 days to create a new habit.

Maxwell Maltz started this myth. He was a plastic surgeon who later enjoyed tremendous success with his 1960 book, Psycho-Cybernetics, which quickly became a staple of the burgeoning self-help movement at the time, selling more than 30 million copies.

Psycho-Cybernetics is right up there with Napoleon Hill's *Think and Grow Rich* and Dale Carnegie's How to Win Friends and Influence People.

In his book, Maltz asserts that it takes a minimum of 21 days for new behaviors to become a habit. This theory was based on observations he had made as a plastic surgeon: It would take 21 days for patients to get accustomed to having a limb amputated, for instance. He also applied this to himself and found that it took a minimum of 21 days for him to form a new habit.

Many of the self-help thought leaders who followed took this at face value and began to incorporate the 21-days number into their subsequent teachings.

But author James Clear wrote in his blog [www.jamesclear.com] that a British health psychology researcher, Phillippa Lally, purportedly debunked this theory in a study of the habits of 96 people over a 12-week period.

Here's what Clear had to say:

"In Lally's study, it took anywhere from 18 days to 254 days for people to form a new habit.

"In other words, if you want to set your expectations appropriately, the truth is that it will probably take you anywhere from two months to eight months to build a new behavior into your life — not 21 days."

Clear reminded us that Maltz said that the 21 days were a minimum.

But this book is not about splitting hairs. It's about results.

At the end of the day, how long it takes to form a particular habit doesn't really matter that much. Whether it takes 50 days or 500 days, you have to put in the work either way.

The only way to get to day 500 is to start with day one – so forget about the number and focus on doing the work. BOOM!

PURPOSE AND PASSION

" *The Purpose of Life is a Life of Purpose.*"

– ROBERT BYRNE

Become passionate about your purpose. Some people wake up and say, "Look at what I can do." Someone else may say, "Look what I have to do." When you find your purpose and passion in life, you will wake up and say, "Look at what I get to do!"

It's about working, playing, and enjoying what you get to do. You see this among entrepreneurs who have found joy in their purpose for living. They are enthusiastic and optimistic every day about what they get to do. You can tell they love what they do and it shows.

What do you love to do? What can you get excited about even if you don't get paid? Do you love something so abundantly that you are willing to do it for free?

They say do what you love and the money will follow. If you can figure out how to make a living doing what you love, you are miles ahead of the curve.

Passion + Purpose = A Life of Abundance!

DREAMS DON'T WORK – PLANS DO

"Don't be pushed by your problems.
Be led by your dreams."

– RALPH WALDO EMERSON

People give up on their dreams because of fear – the fear that they will fail to realize their dreams. A person's dreams, either consciously or unconsciously, will fit within their abilities to accomplish what is possible for them, whether they accomplish them or not. A dream is just a direction. You need to use that direction to prompt action because dreams don't just happen.

Dreaming is just the beginning. It's time to put your plans in motion.

This is your chance to create your ideal BOOM life. Let's create a PLAN.

WRITE DOWN YOUR GOALS

Whatever you choose to write down will happen – with action, purpose, and motivation. It's all up to you. If you don't write it down, it won't happen. Your loss. Write down your goals.

PERSONAL GOALS WORKSHEET

Today's Date: _____

3 Month Goals

_____

_____

_____

_____

_____

6 Month Goals

_____

_____

_____

_____

_____

1 Year Goals

_____

_____

_____

_____

3 Year Goals

_____

_____

_____

_____

5 Year Goals

_____

_____

_____

_____

10 Year Goals

_____

_____

_____

_____

Goals can change. So can your plans. That's okay. Now that you have written them down and are clear on what you want, it's time to go after them.

Make sure your goals are as specific as possible. Make a copy of this sheet and put it by your bedside where you can read it every morning and right before you go to bed. Put a couple more copies in conspicuous places around your home and workplace. Read it with emotion until you can feel it happening, and you can see yourself achieving each goal – living with the rewards and enjoying the successes. If you can't see it and believe it, then rewrite the list so that you can. Do it. Do this now. Take a laminated copy with you wherever you go. It's that important!

CHAPTER 4

Enhancing The BOOM

As I mentioned, when I drop the BOOM, it's always before I am about to do something or after I have accomplished something important to me.

Today, for example, I had to make three phone calls to hotels I had been dreading as I hate dealing with customer service. I had to call because I had left clothes behind at one hotel and my camera charger at another. My job as a professional speaker sometimes puts me in multiple states in the course of a week. So, I am in and out of hotels. I also needed to sort out some things with my health insurance.

Dealing with customer service and being put on hold are far from my favorite things to do, but I accomplished what I needed within an hour. After each successfully completed phone call, I dropped the BOOM. I did it: I succeeded. I happily checked that off my to-do list and moved on to the next task.

When you wake up in the morning it's – BOOM! – Clap your hands, wash your face, brush your teeth, and do your dance. Get it done.

BOOM is the kick in the butt to get off the couch. BOOM is also congratulating yourself for your efforts and moving on. BOOM inspires you and applauds you.

Where can you bring the BOOM into your life?

Let's do some work.

JOURNAL INTO YOUR PASSION

Start to keep a journal to figure out what you are passionate about and what truly makes you tick. This time-honored tradition can be therapeutic and life-changing. Try doing this old-school with pen and paper. This will put you in an almost Zen-like state and allow you to relax and see the big picture. Take your time with the process.

I have a few journals I use. One is my daily life with to-do's and tasks. Another is my journal I take to therapy every week. A third journal contains my dreams and plans, business ideas, and any thoughts that come to my head.

Think about the things that used to make your imagination soar when you were a child. Rediscover those long-forgotten aspirations. Reconnect with that sense of wonder about the world.

Write everything down, including the things you are grateful for already. Every day, write down five things you are grateful for without repeating something from the day before. Try it. You'll start being thankful for the smallest of things, and this is excellent. Gratitude is your new attitude. BOOM! I call this kind of journal a Gratitude Journal.

Write without fear of ridicule or judgment from others. This is your sacred ground, your top-secret file, and the blueprint for your life.

YOU ARE YOUR ASSOCIATES

If you play with dogs, you have fun. If you swim with sharks, you get eaten. That simple.

I'm paraphrasing here, but personal development guru, Jim Rohn, used to say that we are the average of the five people we hang out with the most. I believe this.

If your tribe is full of complainers and naysayers, then it stands to reason that this negativity will ultimately rub off on you, robbing you of your effectiveness and taking you out of purpose.

We have all seen old married couples who seem to have morphed into the same person, telling the same stories and taking on the personality traits of the other. Have you noticed that dogs sometimes take on the same temperament as their owners? I have, and I am sure you have, too.

Be careful with whom you choose to spend time with. If your circle of friends brings you down, it's time to make a change. If that change means changing your circle of friends, then change your circle of friends.

Spend time with those who encourage and inspire you, and you will immediately notice the positive upswing in your daily life. Keep people close who are willing to tell you the naked truth and push you toward your goals. These people are your BOOM team of supporters.

Part of your self-esteem and fulfillment comes from being of value to others, so remember – it's not just about what people can do for you - but also what you can do for others. Develop a close circle of like-minded comrades.

If you, occasionally, want to venture out for a night on the town with old pals from school who aren't part of your close circle, no problem – but be sure you know when to buckle down. Do not get sucked into constant time-wasting activities with people you are friendly with, but whom you know will only hold you back.

Keep in touch with loved ones but don't become a guest at anybody's pity party. Connect often with people who are most important to you, and don't forget to be of service to others.

SLOW DOWN

Rome wasn't built in a day and neither are your successes. Keep believing in yourself throughout this process, especially when you feel down or stuck. Success is about consistency; grinding towards your goals and working your plan.

Overnight success takes 15-20 years. Don't get caught up in comparing your life to others. Life isn't a race. You are on your own journey. Remember this: Slow is fast and fast is slow. Think it all through. Embrace it. What's the rush?

3 THINGS YOU SHOULD DO EVERY DAY

When I was a young Marine stationed at Camp Lejeune, NC, I remember watching ESPN's first-ever ESPY Awards presentation, where renowned college basketball coach and broadcaster, Jim Valvano [Jimmy V], received the inaugural Arthur Ashe Courage and Humanitarian Award.

Valvano was dying of cancer, and he had very little time left. He gave his now-famous "Never Give Up" speech, which has since inspired many to give hundreds of millions of dollars to cancer research.

In that speech, he talked about three things you should do every day.

 ### Laugh

Since I'm battling depression, it's hard for me just to laugh. However, I love my friends and family, and when I am with them, I try and be present in the moment. By doing this, I can laugh and feel free.

Laugh often. Laugh with others. Learn to love laughing and feel the joy laughter gives you and the people you laugh with.

 ### Think

I get up at five a.m. because I want to start my day with positive thoughts, affirmations, gratitude, and rewriting my to-do list.

Spend time in thought.

 ### Feel

Be emotional. Be present. Feel. Ask for help. Offer help. Be compassionate. Allow yourself to feel for others and what they might be going through. Allow your emotions to be present. Show empathy towards others.

As Jimmy Valvano said, "Think about it. You do that every day. That's a good day!" BOOM!

We miss you, Jimmy V. Don't give up. Don't ever give up!

FEED YOUR SOUL - EXERCISE, EAT HEALTHY, AND SLEEP

A good exercise and nutrition plan can change your whole life. Once you start exercising and eating better, you'll notice immediate changes in your mood and energy levels.

It's really simple too. Engage in about 30 minutes a day of aerobic exercise and two full-body strength training sessions each week. Don't forget a simple daily stretching and mobility routine.

Eat a nutritionally balanced diet, low in fat and sodium but high in fiber.

The National Sleep Foundation recommends between seven and nine hours of uninterrupted sleep for adults from ages 18 to 64. If you are a teenager, that number was recently widened to between eight and ten hours.

It's not a badge of honor to slog through your busy day in a sleep-deprived haze, and you could make crucial mistakes along the way. Continued lack of sleep will eventually impact your health.

Do yourself and others a favor and try to sleep well every night. This will make you more present as you go through your BOOM day.

ALWAYS BE LEARNING

Our world is one of exponential change. To stay ahead of the curve, it's imperative that you keep learning. Although we have most of the information ever known to man at our fingertips, it's astonishing to me that many people would rather spend their time posting selfies, memes, or cat videos rather than expanding their horizons and their options.

Read. Learn something new every day. Get that degree. Take an online course. Learn a new skill or update an old one. Become an expert. If you have a question about something, Google it and go deep. Learn to play an instrument by watching a YouTube video.

YouTube and Social Media pages are a great place to study successful people and get inspired to learn. Great knowledge and inspiration is all around us. Three of my favorites to follow are: Hal Elrod who wrote the bestseller, Miracle Morning; renowned fitness expert and life-coach, Chalene Johnson; and Gary Vanderchuk, who doesn't need an explanation. These are three kick-butt people to follow on Social Media. Also, Eric Thomas, motivational guru, and Simon Sinek, who is a straight up genius and so articulate in how he explains things. These people are change agents in the game of life! BOOM!

Another change agent who's been around for nearly a quarter of a century is success guru Anthony Robbins.

Author and broadcaster, Earl Nightingale, once said that one extra hour of study per day would make you a national expert in five years or less. What are you reading and studying that can make you an expert in less than five years?

You are learning right now. Always continue to learn. Always be better.

CHAPTER 5

You Are Not Your Mistakes

All your mistakes add up to absolutely nothing, but they can be educational. Now you know what not to do.

We have all made mistakes and our mistakes have taught us some pretty great lessons. Do you agree?

I have made my fair share of mistakes too, but I don't want to live my life despairing over how I could have done better in so many ways. I don't want to spend the rest of my life beating myself up.

When life knocks you down, you get back up and push onward. This has been one of my core messages in my 25 years of motivational speaking. You are not the culmination of the mistakes you have made. You are not who you were five, 10, 15, or 20 years ago. You are not who you were in that long term relationship that didn't last. You are not who other people think you are now when they knew you then.

Opinions of others who are not in your immediate circle mean nothing, and should not impede your progress on life's journey. Keep your own counsel, but pay attention to the constructive advice from your family, your teachers, coaches, and trusted friends. Most importantly, how God sees you and how you see yourself is what really matters most.

Move onward from your past and look to the future with great optimism.

Motivational giant, Zig Ziglar, said that your attitude, not your aptitude, will determine your altitude.

You either wake up and choose anger, hate, resentment, jealousy, and bitterness, or you choose kindness, love, generosity, gratitude, and unselfishness. It's all in your attitude. Remember reading that earlier? Important enough for me to write it twice. You're welcome.

Choices determine your outcome as much as your attitude. Choose wisely. Choose you. Choose life. Choose love. Choose health. Choose to be present.

KNOW WHO YOU ARE

To know who you are is to know who you are not. To know who you are is to also accept that you may never be who you want to be. Don't live your life today for who you hope to be down the road because down the road things change. We change. Know who you are now and be comfortable with who you are not.

We are constantly working on being better. Know who you are and know where you are headed.

My goal is to be comfortable with who I am – not who others want me to be – and strive to constantly be the person I someday hope to meet.

BOOM!
Time for a break!

She Accepts Me . . . I'm not easy

Sugar Bear . . .
My sunshine!

I'm a different speaker today than I was 10 years ago. Loving this new lease on life. BOOM!

She makes life all better.
Life in South Carolina.

Follow my VLOG - BOOM

I've lost 80 lbs. Free of Diabetes. Got a
new lease on life. Healthy body.
Healthy mind.

BOOM - Podcast and BOOM Facebook page. What is your BOOM?

Home Sweet Home, Myrtle Beach, SC.

My buddy Patrick (Autism). We love Harley Davidson.

When a suicide brings out 2500 community members to listen to you talk about today's youth and Teen Mental Health. WOW!

Road Warrior - Always occupied in thought and reflectio

1,000 miles in 24 hours. I love to ride. My special place - Smokey Mountains.

Smokey Mountains - The Dragon

The single greatest thing I've ever done; I served my country as a United States Marine.

Ockidocki! Let's continue!

CHAPTER 6

Mental Illness Is My Mental Strength

This chapter is for those who struggle with mental health or addiction issues. Accepting and working with these issues is a part of living the BOOM in your life.

I've been in therapy for 25 years. When things are good, I am in therapy, and when things could be better, I realize that I have fallen short on my counseling appointments.

I struggle with mental illness, but my diagnoses have become so significant that I have gained a new perspective on who I am and why I am the way I am. Too many people fight it. You can't fight it. You won't win the fight, but you can accept it, learn from it, and become a great advocate for it. In my journey, I have come to realize that my mental illness is my mental strength. BOOM!

Turning the lens on myself and drilling down on my mental health in my forties has not been easy, but I have come a long way toward understanding and accepting myself. Most importantly, I have truly become aware of who I am and who I am not. I have accepted that I have triggers and when those triggers are hit, I react in certain ways. Dialing in on my mental illness, I have learned how to cope and I have learned tricks to help me through some of the tough times.

I would highly encourage you to ask for help (that's what the BOOM is all about), if you need it and begin your journey on the road to clarity. It's been great for me. I'm proud of myself for not being ashamed of having asked for help during some of the toughest times.

MEDICATION

You need to be your best advocate in order to find the medication that is right for you. Keep a journal of your behavior, emotions, reactions, and the situations surrounding them. Know who you are and how you are responding to situations. This way, when you talk to your therapist, he or she can help you pinpoint what you are dealing with. That is how I became diagnosed with major depression, bipolar type 2, attention deficit disorder (ADD), and post-traumatic stress disorder (PTSD). From there, I was able to meet with my doctor and try out different medications. With the correct combination of medication and cognitive behavioral therapy, I found the perfect mix and continue to stay on this course.

COGNITIVE BEHAVIORAL THERAPY

The BOOM in Cognitive Behavioral Therapy (CBT) in its simple definition is a form of psychotherapy that emphasizes the important role of thinking in how we feel and what we do. Pretty simple, huh? It's not Voodoo or anything spiritual.

The National Association of Cognitive Behavioral Therapists' [NACBT] website states that CBT "does not tell people how they should feel. However, most people seeking therapy do not want to feel the way they have been feeling."

According to the NACBT, one of the goals of CBT is for patients to stay calm in the face of problems because problems come regardless of feelings.

"If we are upset about our problems, we have two problems — the problem, and our upset about it. Most people want to have the fewest number of problems possible. So when we learn how to more calmly accept a personal problem, not only do we feel better, but we usually put ourselves in a better position to make use of our intelligence, knowledge, energy, and resources to resolve the problem."

I decided to add this to the book because of how strongly I believe in therapy and medication. I am also strong in my beliefs that when one with mental illness accepts him/herself and seeks answers, he/she can live a normal life and improve things quickly. Nobody can do it for you. You have to bring the BOOM to your own success and that becomes your mental strength.

COUNSELING IN MY LIFE

I am at the point in counseling where we address different issues in my life, whether that be insecurities about abandonment and rejection, or issues with trust in relationships. What generally happens is that I get to speak about what's on my heart and mind – what I am thinking, what I am feeling – and then my therapist helps me sort through my feelings.

One of the big things to understand is that my therapist doesn't answer these questions *for* me, but she helps me to put things into perspective. We also have such a trusted relationship that she is honest with me and I want her to be. Sometimes I don't see in me what she is hearing in my words. I then listen to what she's thinking and receive clarity for some issues. It takes time to have this trust.

Instead of my reacting to situations, my therapist helps me respond to situations. One of the biggest things I have come to learn is that when you have expectations and expectations aren't met, then you become disappointed – so instead of having expectations, focus more on the objective.

I am writing this chapter while on a cruise ship, and I will use this as an example.

I'm on vacation, so my expectation could be that I am going to relax. I am going to eat good food and work out every day. I am going to be entertained every day – and this ship is supposed to provide all of that for me.

Well, if that doesn't happen and the ship doesn't really provide that – but it was my expectation – then I would become disappointed.

From an objective-based viewpoint, the scenario changes. I get on the ship and find ways to relax. I find the entertainment and the other activities that are going to make me happy. I choose the right foods, and I put myself in the right place. It's all up to me.

That's the objective over the expectation.

These are the little things you learn in counseling. You learn to take time to think before reacting to the situation. You stop – you walk away – and you respond later.

The one thing with my bipolar (type 2) is that everything to me is like a reaction. I get an email, and I think I have to react right away when the reality is that I could just sit back and deal with it later when I am in a better state of mind.

For me, counseling is about awareness and having someone help me think through situations. From a professional point of view, counseling really helps me as I work with my audiences – whether in a group or one-on-one.

ADDICTION AND RECOVERY

So much has been written about addiction that it would be redundant for me to discuss it here, but this needs to be said: If you are struggling with substance abuse or addiction of any kind – there is so much help available, and with each passing year, the stigma attached to addiction and to those in recovery is lifting.

With recovery in the mainstream, society is more willing to give second (or third) chances.

The 12 Steps first outlined by Alcoholics Anonymous has been adopted by countless other groups such as Narcotics Anonymous, Gamblers Anonymous, Overeaters Anonymous, and many more. The plain and simple fact about these steps is that they work.

American Addiction Centers put it this way on their website:

"The 12-Step philosophy pioneered by Alcoholics Anonymous is used by about 74 percent of treatment centers. The basic premise of this model is that people can help one another achieve and maintain abstinence from substances of abuse, but that healing cannot come about unless people with addictions surrender to a higher power."

The 12 Steps work, but, as they say, only if you work them – and they are certainly not the only path to recovery.

For those struggling with addiction, the first BOOM is getting help – but here's the tricky part – you are going to have to get honest with yourself, admit you have a problem and seek help by whatever means possible.

If you are sick and tired of being sick and tired, take that first step and seek help today. Remember: NOTHING CHANGES IF NOTHING CHANGES.

BOOM!

CHAPTER 7

You Can If You Think You Can

NO LIMITS

> *"What the mind of man can conceive and believe, it can achieve."*
>
> – NAPOLEON HILL

Some say, "I can't." Others say, "That's impossible." Many say, "I don't know how."

These are all powerful statements, and you will manifest exactly what you put into place with those words. In fact, Henry Ford put it this way: "Whether you think you can or whether you think you can't, you're right."

Either you think you can or think you can't.

Over the years, many people have called or emailed me, asking me how they can become a professional motivational speaker. What I've come to learn is that I will give them my 10 minutes of time, but that isn't really what they want because they won't end up following my advice. What they really want is me to help them along the journey. They want me to do the work for them.

The same goes for people in many fields. Everybody knows the person who has an "idea du jour," almost always coming up with a grand plan and then discarding it when another one comes along. These people have a real problem getting to the actual work to bring these ideas into reality, and likely never will. Somehow, the act of giving voice to these fleeting ideas is enough for them.

As I have said, dreams don't work. Plans do.

What can be and what will be begins with how you first communicate your words to yourself. You must be willing to do the hard work, to figure it out, and to ask the right questions. Most importantly, it is essential for you to communicate an "I can" statement, which essentially means, "I will."

Saying "I can" and taking action means that no matter what the outcome, you have already created a different future from what you are living right now. You have taken responsibility for the direction of your life. You are in the driver's seat.

Those who want a brighter future harbor no thoughts of what might be impossible. They change their words. They take immediate action. They make no excuses. They ask questions and then they ask better questions. They do the research. They find the answers by actively pursuing solutions – and they refuse to stop till they have the answers they want.

There are no limits to what you can do and achieve.

People who dare to dream and take the initiative to act on their plans are possibility thinkers. They think outside the box. They place zero limitations on themselves and what they are capable of. They turn setbacks into opportunities, failures into successes, and keep moving forward.

BOOM!

CHAPTER 8

Keeping It Real: BOOM Authenticity Tips

This above all:

> *"To thine own self be true,*
> *And it must follow, as the night the day,*
> *Thou canst not then be false to any man."*

— SHAKESPEARE

BE TRUE TO YOURSELF

It's worth repeating that if you know who you are, then you should also know who you are not. When you are not clear on these things, you get sidetracked, confused, and lose your purpose.

I should know. This happened to me many years ago as a young speaker, and it almost ended my career.

I wanted to be the best speaker out there – funny, popular, witty – and as I thought at the time, anything other than myself. In one of the stories I shared, I started to include part of another speaker's story. Obviously, this is the last thing you want to do as a professional speaker.

The other speaker, Mark Scharenbroich, is a very popular speaker and probably one of the best in the world.

I did this for approximately six months to a year, and I finally got caught doing it. Mark called me one day, and it was crippling. I felt so guilty, so wrong; like I had no integrity, and so dirty that I wanted to quit speaking. I lost the respect of a lot of people. I lost a lot of friends. I went through a really, really tough time for probably six months. Even to this day, I am still thought of as "That guy!" to many.

I could have given up and quit speaking then and there, but I made the decision that I loved speaking – and if I wanted to be a speaker, if I was going to be any good as a speaker, I needed to be me. I needed to tell my story and have my own style.

I asked Mark for forgiveness, and he forgave me. We have since had conversations. But my defining moment as a speaker came when I realized that I couldn't be Mark or any other speaker. I could no longer be who I was not, and this was the greatest lesson I ever learned personally and professionally.

In the years that followed, I told my own story. I continue to deliver it now with passion and enthusiasm – with energy and earnestness. Because I learned to be true to who I am, my career has skyrocketed. And in that process, I have accepted the fact that as a speaker, not everybody is going to like me – but if everybody does like you, what difference do you make?

When it comes to authenticity, you have to be comfortable with yourself. You are not a carbon copy of anybody else. You are the only one on the rack, and your self-value is really important. You get to create the person you want to be through the people and experiences that are influential in your life.

TIME FOR INTROSPECTION

Go back to chapter 3 and review the section on Purpose and Passion. Also, make sure to review your journal and your goals regularly to make sure that you stay on track.

If you are not happy with your direction at any time, change course immediately.

Using your journal, answer the following questions. I challenge you to answer them honestly:

 ### Is my life meaningful?
Take your time with this. Put this book down for a few hours. Contemplate this question today, and be sure to list your reasons why or why not.

 ### Is my life fulfilling?
What does it mean to you – and you only – to live a fulfilling life? What purpose resonates in your heart of hearts? Dwell on this.

 ### Is my life rewarding?
Are you experiencing joy and meaning in your daily life? Are you making a difference? Get clear on this.

These are significant questions for you to ponder, and the answers can serve as a beacon to guide you in your journey. Did you answer yes to all of these? Some? None?

When you get to the point where you can say, "Yes!" to these three questions, you can change anything in your life. Add the BOOM where you need to. Make a change so you can say, "Yes!"

You are not a tree. You are not fixed in your emotions, thoughts, nor your physical self. Change what you can and make better what you can't. BOOM!

BE TRUE TO OTHERS

At the end of the day, your word is all you have. Protect your integrity at all costs.

Keep your word. It's not "do as I say" – it's "do as I do." If you want respect from others, be honest. Be a person of integrity and good character. Treating people with respect is very important.

Make sure that you are always upfront and honest with those around you, even when you think it doesn't matter. When you say you are going to be somewhere at a certain time, do your best to honor that. If you promise to deliver goods or services to somebody by a certain deadline, make sure that is a priority. If you tell your kid you will be at that recital or sports event, make sure you are there.

If you know that you are going to miss a deadline or appointment, suck it up and let the other person know as soon as possible. Word gets around, and sometimes a failure in this department – as insignificant as it might seem at the time – will have repercussions you don't yet realize.

Show up. Let your handshake mean something. Live by the Golden Rule as laid out in the Book of Matthew: "Do unto others as you would have them do unto you." This transcends religion and will make a huge difference in your life.

Somebody once said that integrity is doing the right thing even when no one is watching. I believe that, and so should you. Whether people are watching you or not, you need to make the right choice. In the aforementioned situations of showing up when you say you will and treating others with respect, you know others will know when you lacked integrity. However, you need to uphold your integrity even when others may not easily "catch" you.

When faced with a tough situation, always choose the hard right over the easy wrong. This will place you head-and-shoulders above those who make excuses, cut corners, or squirm out of their responsibilities.

It's easy to take the shortcut, but in the end, it always catches up to you.

Before my grandfather passed away, he told me that we never seem to have the time to do things right, but we always have time to do things over. Why don't we just do it right the first time? I'll never forget when we had this particular conversation. He was an amazing man.

And while we're talking about being true to others, remember that a kind word or a smile can go a long way. Greet everybody with a smile, regardless of whether you get one back. Hold the door open for the next person, whether they thank you or not.

You never know what the other person might be going through. A little human kindness might just be the spark they need to keep going.

Kindness and common courtesy are essential traits that go hand in hand with respect for one another, respect for your neighbors, respect for your community – and respect for yourself.

KNOW WHEN TO SAY NO

It's easy to get pulled in different directions, and sometimes you will overextend yourself. Learning to say no is about having balance and boundaries in your life and eliminating the stress that you don't need to put yourself through.

People will always want to borrow things or ask you for this or that. Learn to say no – not because you are being a jerk, but because you have balance and boundaries. You know what is right and what is wrong, and you get to draw the line in the sand. Free up some time. You don't have to be everybody or everything to other people.

NOT EVERYONE WILL LIKE YOU

If everybody likes you, are you really making a difference? That's a big thing to understand in knowing who you are and who you are not.

Not everyone will like you. Close your circle. What is important to understand is that when you close your circle, you are allowing yourself to have the right people in your life.

If you have two or three confidants in your life, you are lucky. Those people are part of your BOOM team – the very small group that you keep close.

It's not your job to like me. That's my job.

The world will judge you and critique you every day. Don't judge or critique yourself. Your job is to like yourself. Your job is to work really hard at being the person you would like to meet someday. Your job is to grind every day to put food on your table and to pay your own way through life. Don't get caught up in trying to please the world because the world will try to pull you in different directions.

Concentrate on your circle.

CHAPTER 9

Have Patience With The Process

I met a 15 year old young man while speaking at a high school in upstate New York. He told me that he wanted to be a creator – a creator of entertainment. I wasn't really sure what that meant, but I wanted to listen to his heart more than I wanted to understand what he was trying to do. He shared that his business partner/ friend was frustrated because their successes weren't happening fast enough; they had been on YouTube for six months.

This is part of the problem with today's society: We aren't willing to work long and hard for what we want in our lives. We think that because we invest in something for a while, success is automatic. Investing in something is what we do. Success is what comes as a result of long hours and hard work. Success doesn't have a time limit. Success isn't easy nor is it automatic.

I've been a professional speaker – a motivational speaker – for 25 years. I've endured the ups and downs of failure and great successes. I've ridden the highs and lows. It's been a most incredible journey and one thing I know for certain is that every week I receive phone calls, emails, and private messages on my social media accounts asking how I became successful as a speaker.

The answer? Hard work. Grinding 24/7/365. Sacrifice. Determination. Not giving up. Letting people laugh at me in the beginning. Working through hard times.

Contrary to what many might think, I did not achieve success overnight. It's been 25 years of tough times and achievements. I've driven through the night more times that I can remember. I've flown to Frankfurt, Germany, to speak to teachers for $1000 and paid my own airfare of $1200, which means that I paid them to speak. This doesn't include the cost of food and lodging. I flew to Vietnam. The flight time alone was 30 hours. I was there for three days and flew 30 hours back to the states. I did this for a nominal fee that didn't cover my expenses and time away. I can tell you many more stories where you'd be like, "Jeff, why would you do that?"

There are also the stories where I didn't have to work nearly as hard for twice or triple that money. You take the good with the bad. You do what you need to do. It's called working hard and being thankful for opportunity.

Overnight success can take 15 to 20 years. This is the question I want to ask you: Are you willing to do the little things that others aren't willing to do? Are you willing to show up early and stay late? What are you willing to do each and every day to be successful?

My friends, it's about having patience in the process that will bring you success later. You must understand that. If you are unwilling to be patient and work the process, chances are you will fail, and all you will be left with are excuses.

YOUR SUCCESS LIES WITHIN YOU

I'm about to get real with you. I'm about to significantly drop the BOOM on you.

Tell me the things that you love. Go . . .

You love family, friends, sleep, vacation, cars, California, skateboarding, boats, music, food, concerts – and love itself.

Keep going. What else do you love?

I ask this question every day and you know what nobody ever says? I never hear, "I love myself."

You have got to value yourself more than anything else. Love yourself and this journey you are on. Believe in yourself whether you are 15, 55, or 85. Love yourself.

I think one of the greatest problems with people today is their fear of the unknown, their lack of self-confidence, and their lack of personal responsibility; they're living every day wondering what other people are thinking.

I have three things I attribute my success to:

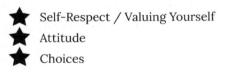

★ Self-Respect / Valuing Yourself
★ Attitude
★ Choices

These are the same three things I wish I knew when I was young that I know now. Don't complicate the process. Respect yourself more than any person, place, or thing. Believe in you.

Self-Respect/Valuing Yourself

Listen – when you go home and look in the mirror, if you don't like that reflection looking back at you, don't blame it on the mirror. It's not the mirror. It's you, and that is where you start. You start by fixing what you think about yourself when you look in that mirror every day. Stand in front of the mirror until you learn to love yourself.

Starting now, figure out who you are. This is also about knowing who you are not. You are not what others want you to be. You are not the opinions of others. You are the opinion of yourself, whether that is good or bad. Own it. Change it. Be it. Work on it.

BOOM!

Know who you are not. Get really in tune with who you are and let that be where you come from. Respect yourself.

Attitude

Attitude is a little thing that makes a big difference. You either think you can, or you think you can't. Either way, you are what you think of yourself.

The Law of Attraction says you will attract what you think about. Attitude says that I am going to be on top of my game every day, grinding as hard as possible, and I am going to love it. As a result, what I put into my day is what I will get out of it. I shall reap what I sow. Attitude is also about being thankful and appreciative for the little things such as the process I work through each and every day

Choices

Never underestimate the power of your choices, and always choose wisely.

Like a pilot with a pre-flight checklist, run through your own mental checklist every day.

I have a choice in how I react or respond to situations. I can choose to be happy or I can choose to be sad. I can choose to be a victim or I can choose to be a victor. I can choose to be bitter or I can choose to be better. I can choose to carry hate in my heart or I can choose to forgive. You have the same choices to make, too.

These are the choices we must make every day.

LIFE HAPPENS *FOR* YOU

You are the sum total of everything that happens in your life. When you were young, you had so many experiences that taught you life lessons, but how you reacted is what significantly shaped you. Today, you are the sum total of how you have responded to your past challenges and successes. As you get older, experience tells you that you should know how to react better, but that doesn't mean you know that you know better. Have you started to take responsibility? Have you learned that each circumstance shapes you, or do you blame your shortcomings and failures on something or someone else without considering the part you played in them? Let me explain further.

Can you see yourself in any of the following situations?

You get into an argument or fight with a friend, and you blame it on them.

You get a bad grade, and it's the teacher's fault.

You get fired from your job, and you blame the people at the job, the boss, the management. It's the wrong company. They're stupid. They don't know how to lead or run a business.

You get in trouble, and it's because your parents are too strict, but you don't consider that you came in after curfew.

You don't get in during the game, and all the sudden, the coach sucks. You ever consider the fact that you don't play because, maybe you suck?

You go through a divorce, and you blame your significant other or his/her family.

STOP. Just freaking stop.

Every time you are about to place blame on someone else, this or that, mom and dad, teachers, bosses, coaches or friends – just step back for a second and realize what is happening. Instead of thinking that this is happening to you, try this on for size: This is happening *for* you.

Remember reading this earlier? It's that important I put it in here twice. BOOM!

Life doesn't happen to you. Life happens for you, and with everything you go through, you come out stronger and better if you allow yourself to learn from your experiences.

Mark Twain once wrote, "When I was a boy of 14, my father was so ignorant I could hardly stand to have the old man around. But when I got to be 21, I was astonished at how much the old man had learned in seven years."

It's incredible how much we see in hindsight. Just like Mark Twain, we all recognize moments when our past perspective was wrong. So take the time to learn from it and move on.

I remember when I was an 18-year-old punk. My mom and dad were stupid. I knew everything, and I was going to be a success. I would go on to spend the next seven years thinking I knew best while I pushed away the messengers. I alienated the adults in my life because I didn't want to hear from anyone. I was bitter and ignorant, and I had a huge chip on my shoulder.

Looking back through the lenses of wisdom and experience, I remember that kid.

My attitude was terrible. I made horrible choices because I didn't value myself as a person. This affected other people too because I married very young.

At 19, I was married with a child and was about to join the military. My dad offered me advice – advice I still remember to this day – but I chose not to listen, and this choice not to listen has affected my life all these years later. I thought I knew it all and had it all figured out.

I went through the shadows of hell. I wasn't a good dad to my first daughter or my second daughter when I was 22 years old. I wasn't a good Marine at first because of what I was going through.

I wasn't a good friend, a good son, or a confident person. I was selfish and scared. Straight up, I was an asshole. I didn't take any responsibility and nothing was ever my fault.

Today, I am the result of this flawed thinking. I wish I could turn back time and give myself a do-over based on what I know now, but I can't. I have to live with who I was then and the choices that I made. I can't regret this because it shaped me and taught me so much. I have such an awesome career as a result of those tough times. I'm also living with the consequences from who I was then, too.

When things are tough and you want to heap blame or bitterness on someone else, immediately stop and remember that this is an experience that is not happening to you. It's an experience that is happening *for* you. The quicker you realize this, the better you are going to be as a result. The outcome will be far better. But, you have to stop and take personal responsibility first.

THE TRUTH LIES IN THE MIRROR

In 2013, I got divorced for the second time from an incredible woman to whom I was married for 17 years. She still holds a very special place in my heart. When we divorced, I decided to go to the mirror and take a really hard look at myself.

Instead of blaming her or her family for the failed marriage, I looked in the mirror and asked myself, "What did I have to do with this marriage not working?" It was a very real experience and what I found out was that my mental illness played a huge part in our failed marriage. Yes, there were certainly other major issues, but I am only responsible for my own actions, issues, and how I dealt with things in the marriage. I can only be responsible for myself, and in being responsible for myself I have discovered my mental health was a bigger contributing factor than I wanted to admit.

So then, I seriously started to address my mental illness. I have to deal with my illness – on a daily basis. Currently, I attend counseling every week, working on me and becoming that man whom someday I hope to meet.

BOOM!

When things aren't right in your life, the first place you should go is to the mirror. Learn to ask better questions. You want to ask the right questions, causing you to place the responsibility on yourself and reflect on how you can make any situation better.

Here are some examples of questions you can ask yourself:

How can I be a better husband or wife?
How can I be a better student?
How can I be a better son or daughter?
How can I be a better friend?
How can I improve my grades?
How can I be a better leader?
How can I be more effective in my job?
How can I create more time in the day?
How can I lose weight?

Ask better questions about your objective and place responsibility on yourself for the outcome. Follow through on the answers you come up with.

Life doesn't happen to you. Remember that. Life happens *for* you and each day, every situation shapes you. If you can only understand that life is a process, you will be so much better off.

Life is not a race. Life is a journey, and every day is a very important part of the process. Each day, lessons are taught and how you respond to them is what will bring tomorrow's successes. Trust in your journey.

BOOM!

A GAME CHANGER FOR LIFE

Embracing the process is going to be a total game changer for you and your life. I can hear you now. You are about to drop the BOOM on yourself. I love it.

When you wake up, hit the floor ready to go. Head to the bathroom, brush your teeth, wash your face, and get ready to do your dance. Wake up with a dream and a plan, and the determination to put that plan into action.

I suspect you have a dream because if you didn't, you probably wouldn't be reading this book.

Be a participant in the game of life. Don't just be a spectator. What is your dream? Write it down. Believe it. See it. Feel it. Taste it. Go after it.

Every day you are working toward this dream coming to fruition. You are striving every day to make today better than yesterday and tomorrow better than today.

You are focused and trusting in the process, right? Good. We are on the same page with a clear understanding now.

During this process, there will be interruptions that can take you out of your purpose and deliver a blow to your ego or self-esteem. Circumstances happen that will affect your life for the moment, the day, a week, a month, or maybe a lot longer if you let them.

Some of these circumstances can be addiction, family struggles, divorce, death, mental or physical abuse, financial challenges, a failed business, being let go from a job – and so many more.

How you respond to these circumstances determines how quickly you get back to living in purpose.

As you move forward in your journey and a situation impacts you, it might set you back for a time, but, again, as I always say to my audiences when I speak, "When life knocks you down, you get back up."

You might ask me how to get back up, and I would say that's a great question.

You have to want to get up. If you can look up, you can get up and get back into purpose. Turn your eyes and your body to where you are focused on going. Make tomorrow a better day.

Life is going to happen. You can't control that, but you can control how you respond. You must choose to be better, not bitter. You must choose to be a victor and not a victim. You must choose to see this as life happening for you because, as you go through life's challenges, you are being shaped and molded into a better and stronger person. Everything you go through is all about the process.

Get back into the game. Go after your dreams with a plan in place.

As you look at your life and how far you've come today from last year, last month, this week, or even this morning, don't compromise your success by allowing yourself to get distracted by fleeting temptations that might promise to make you happy in the moment.

We tend to want things now, but this instant gratification mindset can crush your long-term progress and interrupt your daily grind.

To avoid burnout, set tiered goals – short, medium, and long-term goals. Reward yourself when you reach milestones, but don't linger long enough to become distracted. Create simple, daily objectives, celebrate your accomplishments and small victories – and move on.

Remember to embrace the process. It's about having patience in the process. This mindset is very important to your journey. Every day, you are becoming a better and more successful person.

CHAPTER 10

Loss and Legacy

DEALING WITH LOSS

We are all going to die. The sooner we accept this fact, the sooner we really start to live.

Loss happens. It's a part of life, and that's something you need to understand. Whether you love somebody or something, you must accept the fact that nothing is forever – and that is why you should cherish the special moments that you experience in your life. The reality that I really want to stress here is that everything is temporary. We are not on this planet for a long time, and when we lose someone, we realize how short time is.

The way you spell love is T-I-M-E – so really embrace the time you have with people – with things – with experiences. Life is made up of moments within events, and it's the moments you remember and cherish. Happy people really embrace these special moments in their lives.

Sometimes it seems like you can't move on from your loss, but the surest way through this is to allow the grieving process to do its work. When you experience a loss, it's kind of like you have put all your eggs into one basket, and you are left with questions like, "What do I do now?" or "How can I possibly go on?"

Does loss hurt? Yes, absolutely – and it's going to hurt forever.

I think positive and when one door closes, you've got to pick yourself up and move forward so you can allow another door to open.

There is also a lot of help available through therapy and counseling to help you move forward. But, just remember this loss is the circle of life. The Collins Dictionary defines the circle of life as "nature's way of taking and giving back life to earth. It symbolizes the universe being sacred and divine. It represents the infinite nature of energy, meaning if something dies, it gives new life to another."

Whether it's a relationship that ends, the loss of a loved one, or the loss of a job – you have got to embrace opportunities for future growth. I don't think it's fair to assume that everything is permanent.

BUILD YOUR LEGACY

Building a legacy is doing something that is greater than yourself for the benefit of other people who might be less fortunate – for the betterment of your community, your school, or your town. Building a legacy is doing something that will be remembered and appreciated long after you are gone. It's giving back in a way that you are honored for what you did – whether it was your sacrifices or selflessness in the giving of your money or your time.

Make it your goal to leave something or somebody better off because of your effort – something that will continue to impact others long after you are gone. To do this, you must have a purpose that is greater than yourself – whether that is giving to your alma mater for future generations, building a playground in your community, or giving of your money or your time to causes that resonate within you. You might feed the homeless on Thanksgiving and Christmas or help somebody learn to read. The possibilities for selfless service are endless.

Two things come as a result of this legacy-building: You are serving your community and making it better, but remember also that what you do unselfishly raises your self-esteem and makes you feel good. That is a win-win by anybody's standards.

It's not just about you in this world. It's about what you can do to help make everybody's lives a little better because of your time here.

Start thinking more about the other people in your life. Start thinking about what you can do to volunteer in your community. What can you do to help people in your family? What can you do that is bigger than just the opportunity you are building for yourself?

Live unselfishly and serve a purpose that is greater than yourself because really, life isn't about you!

BOOM! Did you hear that?

Now go out there and live the epically awesome life you deserve to live and make sure you drop the BOOM! often.

Much love my friends!

Your friend,

Jeff Yalden

#BOOM

Made in the USA
Columbia, SC
15 March 2020